BRISTOL

Portrait of a Great City

BRISTOL

Portrait of a Great City

JOHN TRELAWNY-ROSS

with commentaries
by John Sansom

First published in 1999 by Redcliffe
Reprinted and revised in 2003

ISBN 1 900178 52 4

British Library Cataloguing-in-Publication-Data
A CIP data record for this book is available from the British Library

REDCLIFFE
Halsgrove House
Lower Moor Way
Tiverton EX16 6SS
T: 01884 243242
F: 01884 243325
www.halsgrove.com

Printed and bound by D'Auria Industrie Grafiche Spa, Italy

CONTENTS

Welcome to BRISTOL

Bristol defies simple classification by the guide-book writer. The visitor to Bath or York, Oxford or Cambridge, knows more or less what to expect. But Bristol is full of delights for the stranger, and still has surprises for those who thought they knew the city well.

Size matters, of course. Bristol cannot be 'done' in a day or two, nor even three: except, perhaps, by the specialist – the lover of medieval churches, the Brunel enthusiast, the maritime historian, the student of eighteenth-century architecture, the theatre buff; even, towards the end of summer, by the hot-air balloon freak. For the connoisseur of the plastic arts, there's now a sufficient body of sculpture in the streets and parks and on the waterfront to warrant a full-day visit for a serious look at public art. To spend some time in each of the city's museums and art galleries would take a series of afternoons.

But in Bristol the whole is unquestionably greater than the sum of the parts. Bristol's history neatly spans the full millennium. In the year 1000 there was, by the standards of the day, a sizeable community here, with fortifications and its own mint, already engaged in the overseas trade which was to play such a significant part in the Bristol story. In the Middle Ages, Bristol ranked along with Norwich and York for importance outside London. The legacy is to be seen in the city's fine medieval churches. Over 500 years ago, John Cabot sailed from here on his voyage of accidental discovery of America, and it was in honour of a Bristol merchant, Richard Ameryk, that the continent was most likely named.

By the eighteenth century, Bristol was demonstrably England's second city, whose prosperity created the fine buildings and streets we can still enjoy today, and the rare artefacts that grace the city's churches and museum collections. It was a time when Bristol played its part in the inhuman triangular slave trade between England, the West Africa coast and the American plantations.

The nineteenth century saw a decline, relative to the fast-growing industrial cities of the Midlands and the North, but Bristol prospered nevertheless and, even with the ravages of twentieth-century development, can still offer Victorian architecture of a quality and scale to excite the most demanding eye. That century saw, too, a genius by the name of Isambard Kingdom Brunel stamp his mark on the city: with the Great Western Railway and its sheds at Temple Meads, the s.s. *Great Britain* now being restored in its original dry dock and, high above the city, his engineering masterpiece, the Clifton Suspension Bridge.

Down the centuries, and to the present day, Bristol has played its part in discovery, invention and enterprise. The list of superlatives – areas of endeavour in which Bristol can claim distinction – is surprisingly long, allowing me the conceit of writing a small book of fifty significant 'Bristol Firsts'.

Bristol has long been a revelation to the visitor. It features in the diaries of the ubiquitous Samuel Pepys who visited the shipyards here in 1668, recording that his party was given 'good entertainment of strawberries, a whole venison pasty cold and plenty of brave wine and above all Bristoll milk'. Thirty years later, Celia Fiennes was noting that 'this town is a very great tradeing citty as most in England, and is esteemed the largest next London'.

Daniel Defoe wrote in similar vein in the 1720s, while Thomas Cox found Bristolians obsessed with business, 'all in a hurry, running up and down with cloudy looks and busy faces'. For Alexander Pope, Bristol had no civilised company, but he was impressed by the recently built Queen Square, 'which is larger than Grosvenor-Square and well-builded … and the Key which is full of ships and goes half round this Square'. Like other visitors, he was struck by the 'hundreds of ships, their masts as thick as they can stand by one another … This Street is fuller of them than the Thames from London Bridge to Deptford … a Long Street full of ships in the Middle and Houses on both sides looks like a Dream.'

William Cobbett, touring the country for his *Rural Rides*, came across 'a great commercial city in the midst of corn-fields, meadows and woods, and the ships coming into the centre of it, miles from anything like sea, up a narrow river, and passing between two clefts of a rock probably a hundred feet high; so that … you look down upon the main topgallant masts of lofty ships that are gliding along!'

The Avon Gorge was indeed a great magnet for the wealthy tourist, and the Victorian popular novelist, Mary Russell Mitford spoke for them all: 'I know nothing in English landscape so lovely or striking as that bit of the Avon beyond the Hot Wells, especially when the tide is in, the ferry boat crossing, and some fine American ship steaming up the river.'

J.B. Priestley, too, warmed to the city on a visit in the 1930s, with 'all the fine big shops down Park Street, the pleasant villas out at Clifton, and an occasional glass of Harvey's Bristol Milk for nearly everybody.'

Today's visitor will find Bristol as it always has been – a busy, working city which happens to have some of the finest buildings and townscapes in England, with the countryside on its doorstep – a city that cherishes its historic monuments, not as precious relics, but as essential elements in its day-to-day life.

Images of Bristol as it was abound in photographic collections and in the City Art Gallery's astonishing Braikenridge collection of more than 1500 drawings of the city as it looked just before the advent of the camera. But friends in the book business have long asked for a book of contemporary photographs, in colour, to show the best of Bristol as it is today. So here is *Bristol: Portrait of a Great City*. Perhaps it is more of a study than a portrait, for just as the visitor cannot do justice to the place in a couple of days, it is impossible to offer a fully rounded portrait in 180 photographs or so.

The book is divided into loosely geographical sections, not to be used as a guide-book, but to provide a degree of pictorial coherence. There is a logic in the choice and order of illustrations. We start on College Green, with one of the city's oldest buildings: the beautiful, under-rated cathedral which grew from an Augustinian abbey and which boasts some of the country's finest Norman details.

We move up Park Street, dominated by Sir George Oatley's massive University Tower, into Clifton with its architectural glories nestling above the natural wonders of the Avon Gorge. From the lingering gentility of John Betjeman's 'leafiest suburb', we descend to the heart of the city, radiating out from Corn Street with its Exchange and its 'nails', the city churches and great bank buildings – some still handling money, others now dealing in pints and pizzas – and from there into King Street and Queen Square, about to be refashioned to something like it would have been in the eighteenth century.

We then proceed to the waterfront, with its cranes and cobble and warehouse conversions, all evocative of Bristol's great maritime past, before looking at Castle Park, the phoenix which has risen from the blitzed heart of the city. We then climb the medieval Christmas Steps to Kingsdown with its streets of houses built for merchants fleeing the grime and stench of the old city, on to Redland and finally the park lands of Blaise and Ashton Court.

With just two exceptions the photographs have been taken by John Trelawny-Ross, whose wonderful images have graced eight Redcliffe books before this one. We have rarely disagreed about choice of subject or treatment, although we both wish there had been room for more. The limitations on space have meant that much of interest has had to be omitted.

In an enduring portrait of this most rewarding of English cities, John records the grand set pieces, the ancient streets and squares, the historic churches, the waterways and the rolling open spaces around the old city. But with his keen eye, he also notes the unusual and eccentric – here, a Victorian grotesque, there a delightful example of art deco. Not all the buildings in this book are architecturally 'important', but they are interesting and worth a second look: all serving as an invitation to Bristolians to explore their city afresh.

John Sansom

AROUND COLLEGE GREEN

College Green: a worthy setting for Bristol Cathedral greatly enhanced by the closure of a busy road. Alexander Pope, visiting the city in 1739, wrote: 'The College Green is pretty and set with trees ... There is a Cathedral very neat.' The City Council cut down the trees, to give a better view of the twentieth-century Council House, but wiser counsel has since prevailed.

Overleaf Gilt unicorn
on the Council House.

Bristol Cathedral from the south east forms a backdrop to a secluded cemetery garden.

The cathedral's Norman chapter house, dating from around 1150, and probably the finest in England.

The Victorian west front, built to the design of G.E. Street and completed in 1888.

Raja Ramohun Roy was an Indian social reformer who died on a visit to Bristol in 1833. This statue, outside the Central Library, was unveiled on 20 November, 1997 to mark the 50th anniversary of Indian independence. It was sculpted by Niranjan Pradhan. There is a fine memorial to Roy in Arnos Vale cemetery.

'Victoria, Queen and Empress' on her pedestal outside the Swallow Royal hotel. This is the work of the queen's favourite sculptor, Joseph Edgar Boehm, and was installed to mark her Golden Jubilee in 1887.

Rated by many a great masterpiece of the early Modern Movement, Charles Holden's Municipal [Central] Library on the corner of College Green has been compared, more than favourably, with Mackintosh's Glasgow Art School.

Detail of the library's front elevation.

A survival from the original abbey which became Bristol Cathedral: the Norman gateway, with the adjoining gatehouse which was added around 1500.

The sweeping neo-Georgian Council House, designed in the 1930s but, with the war intervening, not completed until 1952. The most interesting architectural features are the Lutyens-inspired pavilions at either end crowned with gilt unicorns by David McFall.

The Hatchet Inn, dating from 1606, seen from Denmark Street. In Regency days it was a haunt of Tom Cribb and other leading bare-knuckle fighters. On the first floor a beautiful plasterwork 'cherub' ceiling runs the whole length of the building.

The art nouveau façade of the former Cabot Café on College Green. This was created by Latrobe and Weston, who also designed the striking 1920s Whiteladies Cinema in Clifton.

Interior of the Georgian House at 7 Great George Street, once owned by John Pinney, a Bristol merchant who traded with the West Indies. The poets Coleridge and Wordsworth met here, and went on to publish *Lyrical Ballads* in Bristol in 1798. Courtesy: Bristol City Museums & Art Gallery

St George's church of 1823, with its Greek Doric portico seen from Great George Street, is now a popular concert hall. Its architect, Robert Smirke, also designed the Covent Garden opera house in London.

Cabot Tower, on Brandon Hill, was erected in 1897 to mark the 400th anniversary of the mariner's voyage across the Atlantic.

Charlotte Street. The houses step sharply down from Brandon Hill to Park Street. The balconies are of richly modelled cast iron.

A classic view looking up Park Street: the Wills Memorial Building, funded by the Wills tobacco family, designed by Sir George Oatley and completed in 1925. 'The smoke from a million gold flakes solidifies into a new Gothic Tower for the university ...' wrote J.B. Priestley in *English Journey* in 1934.

The Lord Mayor's Chapel is said to be the only church in the country owned by a local authority. Inside are notable tombs and effigies, rare medieval glass and fine ironwork by the master Bristol smith, William Edney.

The arcaded front façade of the old Bristol Library and Philosophical Institution designed by Foster and Ponton in 1867. The building later became the University refectory, and is now a stylish restaurant bar.

The gift of Sir William Henry Wills: the City Museum and Art Gallery, designed by Sir Frank Wills, and opened in 1905.

A detail from the remains of the Victorian replica High Cross, which was first erected on College Green and can now be seen in Berkeley Square. The original medieval cross was sold off and now adorns the grounds of Stourhead.

CLIFTON

Bristol's most famous landmark: Isambard Kingdom Brunel's elegant suspension bridge spanning the River Avon. Brunel won the design competition as a young engineer, but did not live to see its grand opening in 1864.

Overleaf Fountain at Victoria Rooms.

The craggy splendour of the Avon Gorge topped by the Observatory. Originally a windmill, the Observatory houses a camera obscura and leads to the Giant's Cave, 90 feet below.

Looking downstream towards the Avon Gorge and Clifton Suspension Bridge: a view much beloved of artists down the years.

Bird watchers eager for a glimpse of peregrine falcons which breed across the Gorge.

Watching the balloons go by: early morning spectators. The internationally famed balloon festival is held at Ashton Court each year. The prevailing westerly winds usually take the balloons across the city.

St Vincent's Priory on Sion Hill. This fine neo-Gothic house was for many years the home of eccentric painter and philosopher George Melhuish. When he died in 1985, the city council declined to accept the house as a bequest because it was difficult to open to the public.

Sion Hill: elegant Clifton houses. Not everyone appreciated the way Clifton was going. In 1799 Lady Hesketh complained that 'the Bristol people have done all in their power to ruin the beauties of Clifton Hill by the number of abominable buildings they have erected all over it.'

Royal York Crescent, reckoned to be the longest in Europe. Work started in 1791, but was abandoned during the Napoleonic Wars and not completed until 1820. In 1801, when there were still many gaps and unsold houses along the terrace, the government proposed to turn the whole into an army barracks, greatly to the dismay of the local neighbourhood.

The houses in Royal York Crescent boast a variety of intricate first-floor balconies. This detail is from that at Number Two, which was once a girls' school attended by Empress Eugenie, later to become the wife of Napoleon III.

The statue of Hercules which adorns
the gardens of Goldney House.

The tower in Goldney gardens. The house was built for the Quaker merchant, Thomas Goldney, in 1720, and is now a university hall of residence. The gardens are occasionally open to the public.

The Goldney grotto: Thomas Goldney brought back thousands of exotic shells from the Pacific Ocean to adorn this Aladdin's cave. It took nearly thirty years, from 1737 to 1764, to complete.

Birdcage Walk, with its canopy of pleached limes, crosses the old churchyard of the bombed Clifton parish church.

The Paragon, perched on the edge of Clifton heights, with spectacular views of the city and the Somerset countryside.

Overlooked by the grander Paragon and Windsor Terrace above, Freeland Place steps gently down to the river.

Dowry Square was built during the first half of the eighteenth century. A quiet corner of Hotwells, despite the nearby whirl of traffic.

The plaque on this house in the square marks the time spent here by Humphry Davy when it was the Pneumatic Institution. With Dr Thomas Beddoes, Davy – later to be famed for inventing the miner's safety lamp – experimented with the anaesthetic 'laughing gas'.

Caledonia Place forms one side of Clifton's most formal terrace settings, facing an identical range of houses across tree-planted gardens. A gap of nearly fifty years gives rise to the change in scale and style halfway down the terrace.

The rugged elevations of Victoria Square. W.G. Grace, the 'father' of English cricket, lived at Number 16 at the far end of the terrace. The nearby Clifton College was a favourite cricketing venue.

'There's a breathless hush in the Close tonight – Ten to make and the last man in!' Clifton College was the setting for Henry Newbolt's famous poem using schoolboy cricket as a metaphor for manly conduct in later life.

The Clifton College memorial to the 43 former pupils who died in the Boer War: St George by Alfred Drury, sculpted in bronze and standing on his Gothic pedestal.

The imposing Clifton Assembly Rooms from the Mall gardens. They opened in 1809 as a hotel, and Princess Victoria stayed here in 1830 when touring the country to meet her (doubtless carefully chosen) future subjects.

Francis Greenway, the architect of the rooms, was convicted of forgery and transported to Australia, where he became known as the father of Australian architecture. A plaque on the building commemorates the event.

Christ Church, on Clifton Down Road: a good example of Victorian Early English architecture.

Two miles to Bristol.

A memorial originally erected by Sir William Draper in the grounds of Manilla Hall.

One of many fine nineteenth-century houses in Clifton Park, built at a time when some preferred a gothic-revival style and others a continuation of the classic.

John Piper's 'Tree of Life' windows were commissioned for the rebuilt All Saints' church partly destroyed in the blitz. Piper had earlier visited Bristol as an official war artist; his painting of the ruined St Mary-le-Port church is in London's Tate Gallery.

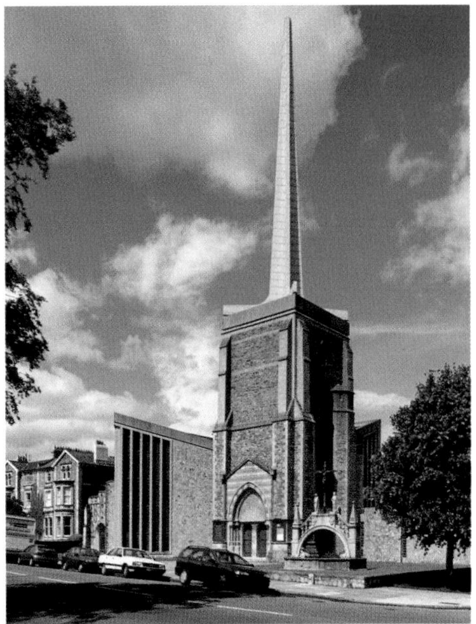

All Saints' church, Pembroke Road. The aluminium spire was pre-fabricated and dropped by crane on to the war-damaged tower below, in the early 1960s.

The Cathedral Church of St Peter & St Paul in Pembroke Road: modern materials for modern times.

The Henry Haig windows.

Looking towards the altar.

Kite flying on Clifton Downs.

Bristol Zoo: an ever popular Bank Holiday destination. It was opened in July, 1836 as the Bristol, Clifton and West of England Zoological Society to promote the study of animals, arboriculture and horticulture. The Zoo, like others, now places a strong emphasis on education and wild-life conservation.

The 'tented' restaurant at the zoo.

A great Bristol institution, the Royal West of England Academy faces the fountain and statuary in front of the Victoria Rooms across the road. It was founded in the mid-nineteenth century with financial help from the mother of the local artist, Rolinda Sharples. A highlight is the Annual Show each autumn.

The Victoria Rooms opened in the early 1840s as a meeting place for Clifton gentility. A popular venue for balls and recitals, the rooms played host to literary luminaries like Charles Dickens and Oscar Wilde.

Edwardian swagger enhanced the classical lines of Charles Dyer's masterpiece. The fountains and sculpture by E.A. Rickards and Henry Poole were added in 1912.

Period survivals: the façade of Edwards Garage in Alma Vale Road and, a reminder of the heyday of popular cinema, the Whiteladies Picture House.

HEART OF THE CITY

In Corn Street, John Wood's Exchange of 1741-43, with the Georgian tower and cupola of All Saints' church.

Overleaf Bristol's finest door hood, in Tailor's Court (off Broad Street), dates from c.1700. Close inspection reveals John the Baptist's head on a platter.

The Corn Street market.

One of four seventeenth-century 'nails', the bronze pillars outside the Exchange, used by merchants to pay cash 'on the nail' and among England's rarest pieces of street furniture.

A monument to Victorian over-confidence: now occupied by Lloyds Bank, this spectacular edifice was built for the West of England & South Wales District Bank, which failed in 1878, ruining most of its shareholders. Its design by W.B. Gingell and T.R. Lysaght drew its inspiration from the Library of St Mark's in Venice.

The intricately sculpted figures by John Evan Thomas represent various imperial and commercial interests; the frieze depicts boys receiving, paying, storing and coining money and printing notes.

Businessmen met in the Commercial Rooms for over 150 years. John McAdam, the road builder, was the first president in 1811. The three statues represent the city, commerce and navigation. Declining membership led to closure and an award-winning pub conversion.

Passing the time of day: HSBC Bank clock tower on the corner of Corn Street and Small Street and, right, the striking quarter-jacks on Christ Church, c.1740, marvelled at by the poet Robert Southey as a young boy.

A delightful entrance to a 1930s office building in Corn Street, formerly insurance offices now an Italian brasserie. The stone figures – *Benevolence and Prudence* and *Peace and Plenty* – are by the noted classical sculptor Hermon Cawthra, working with architect Sir Giles Gilbert Scott.

THE ITALIAN BRASSERIE

The former Prudential Building in Clare Street: Alfred Waterhouse's 1899 design lifts the spirit with its rich terracotta, Dutch gables and turrets from the Loire.

The garden of St Stephen's church: a haven of peace in the busy city. Notables commemorated in St Stephen's include Martin Pring, explorer, Edmund Blanket, fancifully credited with having 'invented' the blanket, and George Macready Chute, theatre manager and comedian.

The former *Bristol Times and Mirror* offices in St. Stephen's Street, built in the Arts and Crafts style at the beginning of the twentieth century.

St Nicholas Market, behind the Exchange: a mix of stalls, pubs and restaurants.

Albion Chambers, Small Street: home to Bristol barristers.

St Nicholas church from Redcliffe Backs. Gutted by Hitler's bombs, the church now serves as Bristol's tourism centre; below is a fine medieval rib-vaulted crypt with a monument to Alderman Whitson, founder of Red Maids' School. Bristol Bridge, for many years the lowest crossing of the River Avon, is just visible on the right hand side of the picture.

An ailing monarch: The Victorian drinking fountain in St Nicholas Street.

The sign of the Elephant pub in St. Nicholas Street. A deed of 1787 suggests that the Elephant replaced an earlier tavern on or near the same site.

A little-known gem. The Italianate-style Stock Exchange building in St Nicholas Street, paid for by entrepreneur Sir George White and completed in 1903. Stockbrokers and jobbers dealt 'on the floor' in local stocks, specialising in tramways, railway, brewery and tobacco shares.

Timothy Mowl has described Henry Williams' design as suggestive of 'a high class bordello patronised by Ronald Firbank'.

Broad Street looking towards St John's Arch, the city's only surviving medieval gate, with the tiny church of St John built onto the original wall. Queen Elizabeth I passed through here on her visit in 1574.

Grotesque ornament in John Street.

Designed for the visionary printer Edward Everard, this tiled façade commemorates Gutenberg, the fifteenth-century printing pioneer and William Morris, the artist-craftsman who helped revive fine printing in the late nineteenth century. The detail shows the central figure, the Spirit of Light. Police had to control the crowds which flocked to Broad Street for the opening in 1901.

Looking up Broad Street towards the Grand Hotel and Christ Church.

Christ Church's classical interior, with its graceful Corinthian columns and ornate ceiling. It was a product of Bristol's eighteenth-century prosperity, and largely the work of local architect William Paty.

Victoria Street, once called the ugliest street in Europe, was built to link the railway terminus at Temple Meads to the city centre. Most of its buildings were destroyed by Hitler's bombs and post-war developers. The Talbot Hotel, close by Bristol Bridge, was turned into offices, and later still given a facelift in the 1990s.

Edward Colston's statue on the Centre, by John Cassidy, was erected in 1895. Another, more youthful, memorial by Rysbrack can be seen in All Saints' church. The city's bells tolled for 16 hours when Colston's body was brought back to Bristol in 1721.

An art nouveau detail: a dolphin was said to have saved Colston's life at sea, and a charitable society of this name was one of three set up to continue the benefactor's work.

Colston Hall: the city's largest venue for entertainments from pop concerts to keep-fit displays.

Number One Bridewell Street: cool elegance in a drab corner of the city.

Contrasting faces of the modern city: the Spectrum offices that greet the visitor arriving from the M32, and a detail from the Post & Press newspaper offices in Temple Way.

KING STREET AND QUEEN SQUARE

Overleaf From the Merchants' almshouses in King Street.

The Theatre Royal in King Street, the oldest working theatre in the country, was described by David Garrick as the most beautiful in Europe. The owners were denied a licence to perform plays, and to circumvent the law the opening on 31 May, 1766 was billed as 'a concert of music interspersed with specimens of rhetorick'.

The Llandoger Trow, c.1665, takes its name from the Severn trows, small sailing ships which plied between Llandogo in the Wye Valley and the Welsh Back quay nearby.

Number Seven King Street, speculatively built to last a life time, but still here over 300 years later.

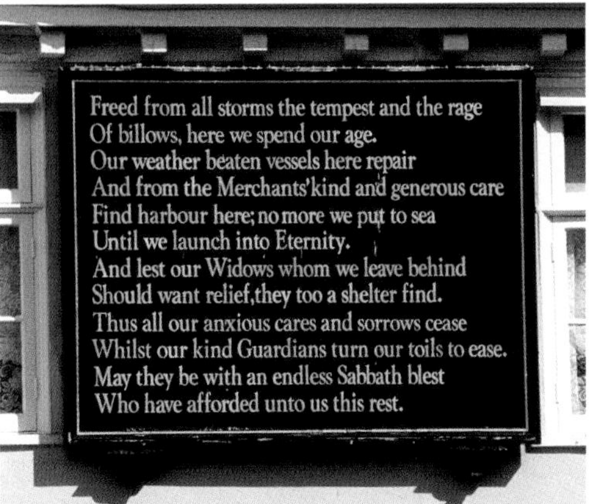

The Merchants' almshouses were founded for retired sailors. The present building dates from 1696, but was partly destroyed, along with the Merchant Venturers' Hall, by enemy bombs in the Second World War. Generations of 'old salts' have ended their years here, swapping yarns about their seafaring exploits.

Terracotta panels from the series of fifteen by Philippa Threlfall on Broad Quay House.

In Queen Square, Rysbrack's statue of William III dressed as a Roman emperor is reckoned the finest equestrian statue in Britain. Dating from 1736, it was commissioned by an ambitious mayor and council to help raise the city's status. The statue forms the centre-piece of the restoration work which has returned a now largely traffic-free Queen Square to its eighteenth-century calm.

Number 29 Queen Square after meticulous restoration. The house survived the mayhem of the Bristol Riots in 1831, when drunken mobs destroyed the Mansion House and much else in the square.

ON THE WATERFRONT

The Floating Harbour looking east towards St Mary Redcliffe church.

Overleaf Pero's Bridge over St Augustine's Reach.

St Mary Redcliffe, famously described more than 400 years ago by Queen Elizabeth I as 'the fairest, goodliest and most famous parish church in England'.

This popular waterfront pub is said to have originated the saying 'as happy as a sand boy'. Young lads despatched to collect sand from the nearby Redcliffe caves to spread on the bar floor were doubtless more than happy to be given free beer for their pains.

Surviving Victorian polychrome brick-work: the former Robinson's warehouse (1874) facing the Bathurst Basin.

Looking across to Redcliffe Backs from Welsh Back: a mixture of new buildings and warehouse conversions retain the scale of the historic waterfront from Bristol Bridge to St Mary Redcliffe.

The Welsh Back waterfront is a popular rendezvous. Nearby offices have been converted into student accommodation.

Bristol's most celebrated Victorian warehouse: Ponton and Gough's red-brick 'Bristol Byzantine' granary on Welsh Back. The home of Avon Cities jazz in the 1970s, the lower floors now house a Belgian café-bar.

The distinctive lines of the former WCA warehouse on Redcliffe Backs, now converted into flats.

Dubbed 'a beer barrel atop a concrete pole', this now-redundant shot tower is a striking land-mark near St Philip's Bridge. The shot-making process of dropping molten lead from a height was invented by a Bristol plumber, William Watts, in 1782. The idea is said to have come to him in a dream. He achieved the optimum height by adding a 50-foot tower to his Redcliffe house, since demolished for road widening.

Bristol's leaning tower: Temple church, just off Victoria Street, was gutted in the Second World War, but the tower had already been at an angle for 550 years after being built on weak foundations.

Arnolfini: contemporary arts in a former tea warehouse. This imaginative conversion in the 1970s heralded new uses for redundant buildings in the once bustling City Docks.

Pero's Bridge: the new walkway linking the Narrow Quay waterfront with the Harbourside arts and science complex being developed on Canon's Marsh. The large 'funnels' are counterweights to raise the bridge when necessary.

The John Cabot bronze by Stephen Joyce outside Arnolfini.

Dockside cranes by the Industrial Museum. In 1970, there were still 42 in the floating harbour, forming a unique skyline; a handful have been kept as reminders that for centuries ocean-going vessels have sailed and steamed right into the heart of the city.

The 35-ton Fairbairn steam crane, built by Stothert & Pitt in 1876, is now preserved for its historical interest.

Millennium Square, on the site of a former car park, is a major waterfront attraction for visitors, with a hands-on science centre, planetarium, botanical house and Imax cinema

The stainless steel space-age planetarium

These new retail banking headquarters for Lloyds Bank on Canon's Marsh have provided the bonus of a venue for waterside open-air concerts.

s.s. *Great Britain*: Brunel's great ship, being restored in her original dry dock, has attracted more than three million visitors. In the 1840s, she was the first ocean-going, propeller-driven iron ship in history.

Moored alongside is the replica *Matthew*, which in 1997 re-enacted John Cabot's historic voyage to Newfoundland.

Not far from the *Great Britain*: boat float and Baltic Wharf houses and flats.

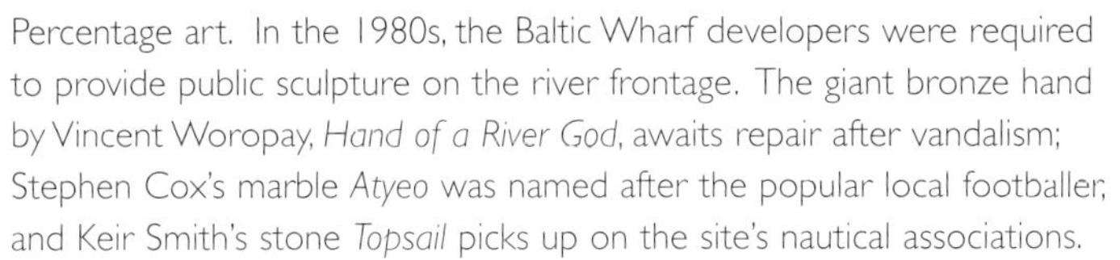

Percentage art. In the 1980s, the Baltic Wharf developers were required to provide public sculpture on the river frontage. The giant bronze hand by Vincent Woropay, *Hand of a River God*, awaits repair after vandalism; Stephen Cox's marble *Atyeo* was named after the popular local footballer, and Keir Smith's stone *Topsail* picks up on the site's nautical associations.

Across the river: new housing on Poole's Wharf, with the Clifton Wood terraces rising behind. The wharf was once used for the coal trade, and for many years was the depository for boats bringing sand dredged from the Bristol Channel.

Within a generation, the harbour has been transformed from commercial to recreational use.

Waterfront housing at Rownham Mead.

Dockside cottages, the clutter of boats and the nearby Nova Scotia pub give a W.W. Jacobs' feel to this stretch of the harbour. Beyond are the Cumberland Basin and the tidal river, with the Clifton terraces and Suspension Bridge forming a backdrop behind.

The Underfall Yard, the maintenance depot for the harbour and the last proper working part of the docks, contains a number of historic engineering artefacts.

CASTLE PARK AND BROADMEAD

Overleaf John Wesley's statue, by C.A. Walker and erected in 1932, recognises that he travelled the best part of a quarter of a million miles on horseback delivering 40,000 sermons.

Castle Park: the ruined St Peter's church has been kept as a reminder of the blitz and as a focal point in the new landscape.

Bristol from balloon. In the foreground are the ruins of the bombed St Peter's church, carefully preserved, in Castle Park which was formed from the devastation of the blitzed city.

The Lower Arcade, Broadmead, 1824, possibly England's finest arcade of its date and type.

Art in the Park: *Beside the Still Waters*, Kilkenny limestone, pennant stone, hedge and lime trees by Peter Randall-Page.

Drinking Fountain, bronze by Kate Malone.

Originally the Merchant Tailors' almshouses of 1701, latterly a bank and now an entrance to the shopping malls of the Galleries.

The New Room, Broadmead, established by preacher John Wesley in 1739 to become the first Methodist building in the world.

Delicate brick sculpture designed and hand-carved by Walter Ritchie at Bristol Eye Hospital, Lower Maudlin Street.

TO KINGSDOWN AND BEYOND

A medieval corner of the old city. Gateway to the former St Bartholomew's Hospital, and the foot of Christmas Steps leading to St Michael's Hill.

Overleaf
David Backhouse's *Cloaked Horseman* in bronze, outside St Bartholomew's House.

Bristol is well endowed with almshouses. In 1483 John Foster, a former mayor, founded these at the top of Christmas Steps, later rebuilt by the Victorians in the Burgundian style, red brick and timber with spiral staircase and ornamental turrets. The adjoining Chapel of the Three Kings of Cologne dates from 1504.

Bristol's most opulent interior: the Elizabethan Red Lodge on Park Row. Dating from 1590, the lodge served John Yonge's Great House where the Colston Hall now stands. Courtesy: Bristol City Museums & Art Gallery

The Royal Fort houses the University's Institute for Advanced Studies. Despite an appearance of being in open country, this mansion by James Bridges is close to the heart of the city. Rococo plasterwork and carvings make the interior the finest eighteenth-century domestic survival in Bristol.

St Michael's Hill, rising from the city centre towards Kingsdown and the suburbs beyond. The road was formerly the principal route to Gloucester. A gibbet stood at the top of the hill.

Colston's Almshouses: one of the great philanthropist's many gifts to the citizens of Bristol, but devalued, according to present-day critics, by his profits from the slave trade.

Somerset Street, built for rich merchants anxious to escape the city and its malodorous harbour. The *Gentleman's Magazine* commented in 1789: 'The suburb called King's-down abounds with good houses; and as this part stands pleasantly in an elevated situation, removed in some degree from the smoke and noise of the city, additions are frequently made to the number of its inhabitants.'

The decorative brick of the former Mission House and Reading Room, near Quarry Steps, the name given to a small area at the north edge of Clifton, where houses were built against a rock face, left after quarry extraction.

Redland church, built originally in 1740 as a private chapel, has splendid busts by Rysbrack and wood and stone carvings by Thomas Paty.

Set in the rolling acres of the Blaise estate, this Georgian Gothic 'castle' was built in 1766 and featured in Jane Austen's *Northanger Abbey*.

Blaise Hamlet: romantic rusticity by John Nash, 1811. The cottages were built by the owners of Blaise the Harford family, for aged persons 'who had moved in respectable walks of life but had fallen under misfortune'. They are now owned by the National Trust.

Kingsweston House, completed in 1719: a grand edifice, crowned by a fine chimney arcade; but one of the smallest houses built by Sir John Vanbrugh.

Ashton Court on the edge of the city; a complex house which evolved over several centuries. The Smyth family, who owned coal mines in Bedminster, lived here for four hundred years, until the house and parklands were sold to Bristol Corporation.